STRAIGHT UP

AMITABH JHA

BLUEROSE PUBLISHERS
India | U.K.

Copyright © Amitabh Jha 2024

All rights reserved by author. No part of this publication may be reproduced, stored in a retrieval system or transmitted in any form or by any means, electronic, mechanical, photocopying, recording or otherwise, without the prior permission of the author. Although every precaution has been taken to verify the accuracy of the information contained herein, the publisher assumes no responsibility for any errors or omissions. No liability is assumed for damages that may result from the use of information contained within.

BlueRose Publishers takes no responsibility for any damages, losses, or liabilities that may arise from the use or misuse of the information, products, or services provided in this publication.

For permissions requests or inquiries regarding this publication, please contact:

BLUEROSE PUBLISHERS
www.BlueRoseONE.com
info@bluerosepublishers.com
+91 8882 898 898
+4407342408967

ISBN: 978-93-6452-305-9

Cover design: Shivani
Typesetting: Sagar

First Edition: September 2024

Contents

Never A Good 1

They Don't Learn 2

We had Hoped 3

My Give Away 4

A Lonely Sound 5

Black and in a Curve 6

Twitter 7

Sundays 8

Struggling in a Party 10

Laws Set by the Frog 11

Late on a Diwali Night 12

The Helpful Recliner Chair 14

Prior to Holi 15

Silent Tea from My Kitchenette 16

Cleanliness of the Crow 17

Saltless on Sundays 18

The Goat 19

Prior to the Meeting 20

Size of an Exhale 21

Early Rains in Delhi 22

They Grow Like Creepers 23

As When You Can't Hide 24

One Bhk	25
Prayer by a Mosque	26
Porcelain Smiles that Aid Me	27
Ganga	28

Never A Good

To raise eyebrows

to lose support

I stop being good

as people and persons

make attempts

to corner

the goodness

of the world

and rob me of my share

to bereave me

in parts

in my own

backyard

They Don't Learn

I found them
their teeth
they relished
oblivious
I never begged for
a pardon
when anointed
with sin and shame
by the happy
snears
seated so near to me
I never turned back
nor cried for help
but waited
they
take a long time to learn

We had Hoped

Underneath the spray

of the sparkling stars

I moan

you

on my terrace

your open arms

that embraced

the last hope

when we met

in attempts to

clinch love

from such an easy world

My Give Away

At the age of twelve
for groceries in bags
I bargained
a chowk bazaar
for items
at the best price
But I learned
not a thing
and grew up unaware
into a haggle
that never tried
to give it away

A Lonely Sound

Very early in the morning
I laid him to rest
and the hirsute head
dropped on the bed
It was my breath alone
that made the sound
But I couldn't stop
looking at the
brown skin
of this face
that just ceased
to reflect what I always
thought was mine
and that no more
breathes back to me.

Black and in a Curve

A very black
set of eyes
and eyelashes
likewise
arranged in a curve
invite a fall
into pleasure
in the night
but who then warns
an aqueous white
without any sign
and unexpressed
cautions
against a tiring sight

Twitter

Seated on the branch
and set to soar
to flap its tireless wings
against the endless sky
her wont to chirp
while in her flight
free to twitter
tiresome sounds
in a ceaseless search
of worms
thoughtful and silent
mostly single on her perch
the summer heat
now soaring high
gasping for breath
not willing to fly
no assistance
and little help
a laborious life
with flapping forelimbs

Sundays

Sunday morning
Eleven o 'clock
Sun breaks on my balcony
The soap opera is on

Digital voices that
capture life and passion
permeate my house
as I move
from kitchen to balcony,
wading through
air alive with
passions wafting on the waves.
I move
from balcony to the living room
caring for my hunger and dirty clothes.

In between
I stare on the sun
In my balcony,
not moving, relieved.

Digital surrogate of emotions
the soap data base
gives me a chance
for all my food
and cauterized moments
in my household.

Struggling in a Party

In a party
thrown in reception
of the bride
at the groom's place
I am struggling
with the eating plate
mounted on the napkin
to serve myself
with food of variety
for my consumption
and then to decide
on the corner
befitting
affiliations
derived from power
politics and connections

Laws Set by the Frog

Wetter in the July rains
no more comfortable in the
overflowing drains
The bull frog emerges
out in the open
leaping long
by the propellant
stretched out hind legs
catching its breath
in a near standstill
but observant
ogling eyes scared of death
a portrayal in theatrics
for a breakfast
of insects no less than six
and spotted skin
clothed upto the chin
when it rests after the hop
for an intellectual pause

Late on a Diwali Night

The other day
after a fulsome meal
in an open air restaurant
and then down the ramp
with a sure
and paid up satiety
on to the road
where nightlife
amidst smell of sweets,
fumes of petrol
and crackers
for a smog
that steeps
statistics of still births.

On roadsides
by now
in tatters
some human forms
attempt to rub
the night sky

and obliterate
fears and fumes
and the scent of crackers.

Sunk in their gaze
some pair of eyes
hush hush a town
so used to its ways.

The Helpful Recliner Chair

Look
before I leave
I will have packed up
the mess
mine that belongs
to me
and for the last
and final
food and drink
talk and laughter
I will depend
on the vibes
in the air
and the comfort
derived from
the recliner chair

Prior to Holi

Prior to Holi
I am coloured
in a washable manner
and await the final
coloring of an
enduring kind
on the Holi day
when joy translates
into colours
and narrow sectarian
ill will and hatred
of the neighbour's
drips down in waters
and colours remain for into the joy.

Silent Tea from My Kitchenette

Its my life
and no freedom
the early morning breakfast
post the diabetes
pink coated pill
on an empty stomach
prayers and God
consigned to the backseat
work and assignments
of the day at hand
rise up like a phantom
but then I make attempts
and further freedom I seek
in teacups
prepared in the still sleeping
almost dark kitchenette
so families
around my government quarter
do not for a bit
find interruptions
and no one in this part is any wiser

Cleanliness of the Crow

Every now and then
the scavenger black crow
rummages it's feathers
with the blacker beak
and then pauses
and the agile head
on the grey girdled neck
attempts to assess
the mammoth leftover
cleaning task

Saltless on Sundays

This Sunday
different though
from the previous ones
the sun this time fairly white
not tinged in yellow
and as it has been cold
for quite some while
the birds and the squirrels
seem to gain warmth from it
and I too remind myself
of a salt less food regime
and special Sunday prayers
to make hay while the sun shines
to remain saltless on Sundays

The Goat

Unopposed walks
the huge black goat
no enemy in sight
it sways its belly
on either side
and the belly
is contained
with kids
that would spring out
soon to cavort
on the mother earth
and with such tender
black coated fur
would dangle their long ears
to join the party
again unopposed

Prior to the Meeting

I wake up
for encounters
with opinions
that vary
and that I detest
I approve
every talk
and decision
and for the sake of
the noise of
a cup of tea and the saucer
I make adjustments
to climb up the
business ladder

Size of an Exhale

Can I attempt
to measure
my devotion
in the innermost
labyrinth
of my cerebral mass
No I cant
but I measure
the length of the exhale
of my breath
when after
 my early morning prayer
I fancy
the length of my exhale
will speak and tell the tale.

Early Rains in Delhi

During the first
Unannounced rains
that blackened the roads
of central Delhi
I noticed through
the tough window panes
of the city bus
en route to Okhala
the continuing struggle
of the gentry
this time caught unaware
and without an umbrella
this was a gentle shower
it did not entirely wet
the clothes or the body
and the two smoking youthful males
when under the parasole
hurriedly they met
and hastily over laughter
recounted all their funny tales

They Grow Like Creepers

When you see
the children grow
like creepers
clawing tender spiral
on your body your person
for support
you make allowances
for the cherish
of a future
that you believe
will be a betterment
and the spawning creeper
so keen to rise
head and shoulders above
the support
you turn back to wonder
you have made a beautiful surrender

As When You Can't Hide

A very criss crossed shirt
doesn't hide at all
the grief within
those brown lines
criss crossed with yellow
the very first button
vigorously left open
to conceal a plight
but the stare of unmoving eyes
and a failure to engage in
most current city gossips
very inadvertently
but surely
reveals
a hounded, and hammered
criss crossed sight

One Bhk

Out of concern

for the safe drinking water

I get installed

a twenty thousand odd

reverse osmosis

electric water purifier

and procure glasses

from the nearby mall

 to eat drink

and make merry

after hosting some old time friends

who kindly enough

accept to fit into

the near slum where I stay

a house without terrace

my one BHK

Prayer by a Mosque

Near the mosque at the roundabout
at the gate a beggar a bag of bones
white torn muslin and mostly dirty
blind, weak and famished might just be sixty
a round metal his begging bowl
held mostly by the left above his knees
regular holes in the cap on his head
regularly the mosque five times in a day
awakens to whispers over open palms
the weak beggar squats at the masjid gate
he downs the begging bowl he can find
a communion of a prayer of a purer kind

Porcelain Smiles that Aid Me

After the office
and the traffic rush
I am back to where I belong
on the bed I lay myself straight
along with the cup and plate
and drinking glasses
my enlisted friends
that have waited for the day
to cheer me up
and give me looks
from the porcelain surface
whenever I ask and when I say.

Ganga

Born in the primordial
its umbilical
tied to the heavenly
shining sheets of ice
it descends
for faithful worshippers
through mammoth black rocks
and mighty gorges
hitting hard and creating sounds
that subdue
the conversation of the onlookers
and reaches the plain
with soil deposits in the belly
now in a slowed down and tempral
allowing the captivated worshippers
on either side of its flank
in the cradle of a clime
when temples all along
built of ancient rocks
and fragrant with freshly plucked flowers
and a sprinkling of the holy ganges water.

www.ingramcontent.com/pod-product-compliance
Lightning Source LLC
LaVergne TN
LVHW041643070526
838199LV00053B/3536